1. Leveling up your craft to write a story that lives long after you've left the planet is what some might call a ridiculous goal.

2. You will not tell that story after reading just one how-to-write book.

3. You will not tell that story as the result of taking one seminar.

4. You know creating a timeless work of art will require the dedication of a world-class athlete. You will be training your mind with as much ferocity and single-minded purpose as an Olympic gold medal hopeful. That kind of cognitive regimen excites you, but you just haven't found a convincing storytelling dojo to do that work.

5. The path to leveling up your creative craft is a dark and treacherous one. You've been at it a long time, and it often feels like you're wearing three-dimensional horse blinders. More times than you'd like to admit, you're not sure if you're moving north or south or east or west. And the worst part? You can't see anyone else, anywhere, going through what you're going through. You're all alone.

WELCOME TO THE STORY GRID UNIVERSE
HERE'S HOW WE CONTEND WITH THOSE TRUTHS

1. We believe we find meaning in the pursuit of creations that last longer than we do. This is *not* ridiculous. Seizing opportunities and overcoming obstacles as we stretch ourselves to reach for seemingly unreachable creations is transformational. We believe this pursuit is the most valuable and honorable way to spend our time here. Even if—especially if—we never reach our lofty creative goals.

2. Writing just one story isn't going to take us to the top. We're moving from point A to Point A^{5000}. We've got lots of mountains to climb, lots of rivers and oceans to cross, and many deep dark forests to traverse along the way. We need topographic guides, and if they're not available, we'll have to figure out how to write them ourselves.

3. We're drawn to seminars to consume the imparted wisdom of an icon in the arena, but we leave with something far more valuable than the curriculum. We get to meet the universe's other pilgrims and compare notes on the terrain.

4. The Story Grid Universe has a virtual dojo, a university in which to work out and get stronger—a place to stumble, correct mistakes, and stumble again, until the moves become automatic and mesmerizing to outside observers.

5. The Story Grid Universe has a performance space, a publishing house dedicated to leveling up the craft with clear boundaries of progress, and the ancillary reference resources to pack for each project mission. There is an infinite number of paths to where you want to be, with a story that works. Seeing how others have made it down their own yellow-brick roads to release their creations into the timeless creative cosmos will help keep you on the straight and narrow path.

All are welcome—the more, the merrier. But please abide by the golden rule:

Put the work above all else, and trust the process.

POINT OF VIEW

WHY NARRATIVE PERSPECTIVE CAN MAKE
OR BREAK YOUR STORY

LESLIE WATTS

STORY GRID

STORY GRID

Story Grid Publishing LLC
223 Egremont Plain Road
PMB 191
Egremont, MA 01230

First Story Grid Publishing Paperback Edition
November 2020

For Information about Special Discounts for Bulk
Purchases,
Please visit www.storygridpublishing.com

ISBN: 978-1-64501-036-4
Ebook: 978-1-64501-037-1

For

All Past, Present, and Future Story Nerds

ABOUT THIS BOOK

This book explores the topic of point of view to help you make a solid choice for your story—whether you're just getting started with your current story or you've been writing for some time. Point of view is the most important technical decision we make in our stories, and the third of the Story Grid Editor's Six Core Questions. This global choice affects everything we write and determines the words we use—and not just the pronouns. If the global genre is what a story is about, then point of view is how we convey that story.

We know these decisions are important, but here's the real challenge. It's possible to write a story that technically meets the requirements of your global genre and Story Grid's Five Commandments of Storytelling while creating an unfocused and meandering narrative or one that stays on the surface and lacks subtext and subtlety. This makes it hard for readers to believe the setting, characters, and situation, and the cathartic moment we call the Core Event falls flat. It makes sense that if the vehicle for a reader's journey is not fit for the purpose, we're in for a very bumpy ride.

We don't want that, but how can we avoid it? Better yet, how can we find the best story vehicle for a satisfying ride?

Of course we need to understand the technical choice and what the options are, but we improve our chances of success when we focus on the experience we want to create in the story. The point of view that brings your story to life in the mind of the reader begins with a fitting narrative device, a situation you invent that helps you tell the story. You might say it's a story you tell yourself (and sometimes the reader) to explain the existence of your story. And it depends on your perspective.

In this Story Grid Beat, we'll examine point of view closely so you can see how it all works. When we reach the end of our journey, you'll have a better understanding of how to create a satisfying experience that effectively delivers your story—and makes writing the story easier in the bargain.

1

POINT OF VIEW

Let's start with the basics. What is point of view?

It's the technical choice we're all familiar with—options that are variations on first, second, and third person.

- First Person: I (or we) wrote a story.
- Second Person: You wrote a story.
- Third Person: Alex (or she or he or they) wrote a story.

Any of these point-of-view choices can happen in the past, present, or future.

- Past: I wrote a scene.
- Present: You write (or are writing) a scene.
- Future: Alex will write a scene.

Point of view is also the *vantage point* from which a story is presented. To deliver a reading experience that satisfies, we must understand both aspects of point of view and how they work together.

What do we mean by vantage point? We might first consider external factors like the place and time where someone stands. Internal factors like the language a person speaks or the beliefs they hold about themselves and the world are relevant too. This is what we mean when we say the villain is the hero of their own story. From their perspective, they aren't doing anything wrong. In fact, they're doing the world a favor by dealing with that troublemaker claiming to be a hero. These external and internal qualities of where you stand (or take a stand) determine what you can perceive and the story you tell about it.

What's fascinating is that you can use the same setting, characters, and events to craft very different stories depending on the vantage point from which it's presented. For example, if you want to tell a story from a criminal's point of view, the master detective subgenre of Crime Story (like *Murder on the Orient Express* by Agatha Christie) wouldn't be your first thought. You might choose the prison subgenre (like *Rita Hayworth and Shawshank Redemption* by Stephen King), or a heist (like *Ocean's Eleven*), or a caper (like *Get Shorty* by Elmore Leonard). When you change the vantage point, you change the story, its message, and as a result, the events and circumstances that matter.

The specificity of a story's vantage point is the reason we can't change the technical point of view by changing the pronouns. In fact, the vantage point should inform our decision to write in first-, second-, or third-person point of view. Not the other way around. For example, if we're writing from the vantage point of the protagonist, as in *To Kill a Mockingbird* (Worldview), first-person point of view makes the most sense. If we want to write a story that employs multiple perspectives, as in *The Heart Is a Lonely Hunter* by Carson McCullers (Worldview), some form of omniscient narration is often a better choice.

With these thoughts on vantage point in mind, let's look at the main point of view options from a fresh perspective. First, we need to break them into two groups based on *showing* and *telling*. For the moment, forget the advice to "show not tell" because that's not what we're getting at here. When it comes to point of view, the categories are about the way we present the story through the *effect* we create rather than a technique found in a particular passage.

Telling comes to the reader through a

narrator. It's as if someone or something is collecting, collating, and sharing the events and circumstances of the story. We hear about what happens from someone who is communicating with someone else. *Showing* is more immediate and recreates the effect of being present and observing the events for ourselves. Either option can be conveyed through first-, second-, or third-person point of view.

We'll start with the point of view types in which a narrator *tells* the story.

TELLING POINTS OF VIEW

Narrated stories create the effect of a story the reader hears from someone else. In these stories someone or something stands between the writer and the reader to tell the story. It makes sense that *who* the narrator is and *where* they stand in relation to the events of the story are important considerations, and that's how we distinguish among the types. We'll move from narrators who participate in the story to those on the outside looking in.

First Person

Characters who reside within the story typically convey their tales through first-person point of view. With this point of view, we know *who* the narrator is relative to the story, and we often know to whom, when, and why the story is told. They can be the protagonist, which we call the luminary agent, or a peripheral narrator who tells a story focused on another character. Whether the central character or not, these stories are locked into one point of view, though there are some creative ways to include other perspectives.

Jim Hawkins in *Treasure Island* by Robert Louis Stevenson (Action), Scout Finch in *To Kill a Mockingbird* by Harper Lee (Worldview), and Bridget in *Bridget Jones's Diary* by Helen Fielding (Love) are typical protagonist-narrators who tell their own stories.

A peripheral narrator who is not the protagonist is a useful option when the protagonist isn't the best character to tell the story *because* of their vantage point. They might lack the perspective to present the story on their own behalf or can be difficult to relate to. For example, Ishmael tells the story of Captain Ahab, who dies while pursuing the great whale in *Moby Dick* by Herman Melville (Action). A narrator as witness also works when the writer wants to conceal the protagonist's thoughts. This works well when John Watson tells the world about Sherlock Holmes's exploits in Sir Arthur Conan Doyle's classic master detective stories (Crime).

Despite being locked into a single point of view, the examples show the many possibilities within the constraints, mostly in terms of the form the narrative takes and when the narrator tells the story. For example, the story can be spoken, written, or thought. The narrative might take the form of an implied interrogation ("The Tell-Tale Heart" by Edgar Allan Poe, Horror), epistolary form (*The Curious Incident of the Dog in the Night-Time* by Mark Haddon, Worldview), or stream of consciousness ("I Stand Here Ironing" by Tillie Olsen, Status).

Narrators who are characters within the story can tell about events in the recent past (*Treasure Island*, Action) or distant past (*The Fishermen* by Chigozie Obioma, Status). Some stories allow us to hear from the same narrator at different points in time, like in *To Kill a Mockingbird* by Harper Lee (Worldview). In *The Beautiful Things That Heaven Bears* (Worldview), author Dinaw Mengestu alternates scenes of present and past events to form the narrative structure. Gaps between the main events and the telling allow the narrator to reveal new events and insights that alter our perspective of the past.

Like other points of view, a primary first-person narrative can be combined with scenes of a different point of view if it makes sense within the story's narrative device. Edith Wharton used this technique in her Society novella *Ethan Frome*.

Second Person

A second-person narrative is another option that often creates the effect of first person but blurs the line between the storyteller and reader. These stories put the reader in the shoes of the narrator who tends to be a character within the story. "How to Be an Other Woman" by Lorrie Moore is an example of second-person telling narration. Though written in present tense, Moore's narrator tells us about events she experienced in the past as a way to help herself or the reader understand how she came to have an affair with a married man.

A Note about Reliability: Questions about whether narrators are reliable arise in the context of first- and second-person narration when a character seems to have a tenuous grip on reality. But the truth is every narrator is unreliable to the extent they are unable or unwilling to see clearly, or when it comes to their personal interest in telling the story. They often want to justify or defend their role in the events of the story they tell. For example, we could see Nick Carraway's narrative in *The Great Gatsby* (Worldview) as a confession. He "reserves judgment" and doesn't find a limit to his tolerance until it is too late to help Gatsby. His failure to act on what he observes is a moral failure that contributes to his disillusionment. Narrator reliability reflects their subjective worldview because their actions in telling the story reflect their goals, which are informed by their beliefs.

Third Person

When the events are narrated from outside the story, we're typically dealing with editorial omniscience. With this point of view, the narrator can inhabit any vantage point, time, or place, with access to the fullest possible range of information, from outside and inside any character's experience (not all of which must be revealed in the story). The storyteller provides exposition, regardless of the characters' awareness of it, and occasionally expresses opinions about the events and circumstances in the story. Character thoughts are *told* to the reader by the narrator, often through the use of thought tags (though free indirect gives us a small sample of a character's individual words).

The storyteller could be identified and speak directly to the reader, as in *The Book Thief* by Markus Zusak (Worldview), narrated by Death. But typically, the narrator remains anonymous as in *A Wizard of Earthsea* by Ursula K. Le Guin (Action), *Animal Farm* by George Orwell (Society), or *Death Comes for the Archbishop* by Willa Cather (Worldview).

Omniscient point of view is often used in expansive scope stories that go wide and/or deep, spanning vast geographic areas, large groups of people (*The Heart is a Lonely Hunter* by Carson McCullers, Worldview), or even an entire life (*The Signature of All Things* by Elizabeth Gilbert, Worldview).

A Note about Head Hopping: Head hopping describes a reading experience when the writer hasn't smoothed transitions from one character's internal experience to that of another character. Or we make a big jump in time or distance. The narrative or psychic distance changes so rapidly the reader is pulled out of the story. This often happens when we haven't chosen a specific narrative device and therefore the shifts occur without a story-based reason. A fitting narrative device provides a purpose for directing the reader's attention here or there. When we know the terrain and why we're moving, we're less likely to pull the wheel suddenly.

3

SHOWING POINTS OF VIEW

Points of view that rely on showing create the effect of a story the reader observes or experiences. These points of view have a more objective feel than telling points of view, but the vantage point from which the story is shown is still a vital consideration.

First Person

Characters within the story can *show* their experience through a first-person present-tense narration as we see in *The Hunger Games* by Suzanne Collins (Action). This point of view is similar to the telling version, but it feels like showing because we know what the character knows and experiences as they do. There is no time to present the events as a story for the benefit of another person. This point of view is not often used perhaps because the immediacy can evoke discomfort in readers. The fourth wall we talk about in theatrical stories, which creates a protective frame for the audience, becomes a thin veil, and we're invited to come close.

Second Person

Second-person point of view can create a similar experience of immediacy because the protective frame we usually rely on in fiction is discarded so the reader can be pulled into the story. From the opening sentences of *Bright Lights, Big City* by Jay McInerney, it feels as if we're waking up in someone else's life while hyper-real events unfold before us. We can't actively participate, like in a Choose Your Own Adventure story. But isn't that appropriate for a tale about people whose lives are out of control? The reader gains a new perspective that is hard to achieve through other points of view.

Third Person

Third-person showing comes in two forms— selective omniscience and dramatic mode.

Selective omniscience is third-person showing from the inside out. Like dramatic mode, no narrator stands between the writer and the reader with selective omniscience (sometimes known as close third point of view). But readers can be shown anything the point-of-view character can see or hear, and the writer can reveal a character's internal sensations, emotions, and thoughts. The interesting external limitation is the inability to see the character's appearance unless they look in a reflective surface.

The vantage point here is from within a single character at a time (sometimes this point of view shifts from scene to scene but not within the scene). Even as the writer provides a window into the characters' internal experience, we're *shown* their thoughts in their own words, rather than being *told about* them in the narrator's words as we see with editorial omniscience.

This is a popular point-of-view choice with a great deal of flexibility, even though we're locked within one character's experience at a time. The external story can be expansive in scope like the Harry Potter series by J.K. Rowling (Action) or *A Game of Thrones* by George R.R. Martin (multiple selective omniscience) (Action), but this point of view also works effectively in quiet internal genre stories like *Brooklyn* by Colm Tóibín (Status).

. . .

A Note about Free Indirect Speech: A writer might use small excerpts of selective omniscient point of view within a story whose primary point of view is editorial omniscience. In that case, we call it *free indirect speech*. With free indirect speech, a narrator tells the story, and the vast majority of words in the telling (other than direct speech or dialogue) belong to the narrator. So, for most of the narration, we're told what happens externally and internally through an *objective* third-person presentation. Sometimes the narrator drops us into the mind of the character (a different vantage point) to reveal thoughts in their own words and provide a *subjective* first-person experience. Instead of our being told about their thoughts identified with a thought tag, we're shown their thoughts. Jane Austen employs this in *Pride and Prejudice* (Love Story).

Dramatic mode is a third-person point of view that creates the experience of observing through a hidden camera or of watching a play. Readers are shown what the characters do and say. There is no access to characters' sensations, emotions, or thoughts because they can't be observed from the outside. The internal experience is communicated through subtext.

Ernest Hemingway's story "Hills Like White Elephants" (Morality) is one of the few pure examples. The narrative feels objective because it's what someone could observe if they were in the room. Even the short introduction that sets the scene, a limited example of telling within the narrative, reveals only objective facts about the situation. The meaning we take away depends on our subjective worldview.

This point-of-view choice is useful when the writer wants to avoid revealing motives or certain facts and when they want to address a topic without discussing it directly. We see modified forms of dramatic mode in Shirley Jackson's "The Lottery" (Horror) and in passages within *Murder on the Orient Express* by Agatha Christie (Crime).

Dramatic mode can be hard to pull off, and it forces the reader to work a little harder to bridge gaps other narratives would normally cover. As a result, we find this form only occasionally in short stories. But even if it's not a great fit for your current story, it's worth practicing. As storytellers, we need to master subtext and learn how to reveal enough but not too much information. This point of view forces us to find creative ways to communicate meaning and to be precise.

4

MULTI-PERSON NARRATIVE

Some writers use multiple points of view within the same story. The truth is we have great flexibility so long as we have story-based reasons for our choices and are mindful about how we apply them. Stories with multi-person narratives tend to be complex with several subplots and smaller story threads. It takes a master craftsperson with lots of practice to execute these moves well, but they allow readers to receive complex narratives that accurately reflect our complicated world. A specific narrative device will be your trusty guide here.

First-person point of view can be presented serially or as part of a collection of different perspectives. *As I Lay Dying* by William Faulkner (Morality) includes narratives from multiple characters, some in first and some in third-person point of view. In *Complicity*

(Thriller), Iain Banks employs a first-person narrative for the protagonist, journalist Cameron Colley, but the villain speaks in second person. When an epistolary narrative device is used, you may see similar combinations, including in *The Guernsey Literary and Potato Peel Pie Society* by Mary Ann Shaffer and Annie Barrows (Worldview) and *Fried Green Tomatoes at the Whistle Stop Cafe* by Fannie Flagg (Worldview).

First person framing stories can include other first-, second-, or third-person narratives to provide additional perspectives. In *A Tale for the Time Being* by Ruth Ozeki (Worldview), we read the first-person narrative of Ruth, a novelist living on the West Coast of Canada, who discovers the first-person narrative of Nao, a girl living in Japan. Ruth rethinks her life and work while she seeks to learn of Nao's fate. Other examples include *Frankenstein; Or the Modern Prometheus* by Mary Shelley (Horror) and *Ethan Frome* by Edith Wharton (Society). Death in *The Book Thief* by Markus Zusak (Worldview) employs first person point of view to address the reader occasionally while dropping into selective omniscient for the main narrative about the protagonist, Liesel Meminger. The overall effect is that of editorial omniscience.

In *Harry Potter and the Half-Blood Prince* by

J.K. Rowling (Action), a story primarily presented in selective omniscience, one scene is presented in dramatic mode. This occurs in chapter two, "Spinners End," a scene where Severus Snape meets with Narcissa Malfoy and Bellatrix Lestrange. We observe their actions and speech but don't have access to the characters' internal experience. This provides two forms of narrative drive: dramatic irony (because we know something Harry doesn't know) and mystery (because we don't know the meaning of Snape's actions). The opening scene of the story is presented in editorial omniscience and features a meeting between the muggle prime minister and the former and new ministers of magic.

Again, this is high-level play. The combinations make sense when the writer has chosen an overarching narrative device that is consistent with all point-of-view elements and makes sense in the story. Before committing to a choice like those identified here, we should understand why we're doing it and what we gain and lose. We need a masterwork to guide us and lots of practice.

5

NARRATIVE DEVICE

We have so many great point-of-view options to choose from when we write a story. That's wonderful, but it can also be overwhelming, especially when we're not sure how to choose. What's our first step?

We must realize that our point-of-view choice causes effects that simulate human experience, and those effects can support the story or not. We need to figure out what experience is the best fit for our story to create a smooth reading journey. How do we do that? If we think about the idea of a vantage point, we're on the right track.

We increase the probability of delivering a satisfying experience (and an easier writing process) when we choose a specific narrative device that is aligned with the global content genre. Remember a narrative device is a story or situation that provides context for your point-of-view choice. It makes it make sense. The protagonist is the person whose story you want to tell, but the narrative device is all about the best position from which to deliver that story. To begin to work this out, consider the following questions.

- Would it be better to show or tell the story?
- From whose perspective or what vantage point is the story best revealed?
- Who is the audience, or who could the audience be?
- Why is the story being told or shown?
- When and where is the story being told or shown relative to the events of the story?
- In what form? Should the experience be one of a written account, spoken narrative, or an internal monologue?

Useful answers to these questions might not appear right away, but writers who review masterworks and keep asking the questions tend to cultivate insights that solve the seemingly impossible problems they face with their stories.

Understanding the *why* of the narrative seems to be key because we can connect it to the global genre through the controlling idea. The controlling idea of a story is a simple cause and effect statement about the change that happens when the protagonist goes through a particular kind of experience. And we receive this distilled message as knowledge when we read the story.

If the story has a narrator, the controlling idea can be the narrator's purpose when they begin telling the story. This is especially the case when the narrator relays events from the distant past. When the narrator is also the protagonist, the controlling idea can be the lesson that flows from the narrator's experience of telling the story.

When the story is shown, our inquiry is a little different because we look to the nature of the specific vantage point for what it is uniquely positioned to reveal. For a basic practical example, consider that a CCTV camera is uniquely positioned to convey a story and message different from but similar to the story and message we might derive from a phone's video recorder.

You can't be expected to accept this at face value, so let's look at some specific examples.

6

BRIDGET JONES'S DIARY

Bridget Jones's Diary is a global Love Story by Helen Fielding. In the story's inciting incident, Bridget meets Mark, who is a great partner for her, but she must gain self-respect before she can realize it and gain authentic love and commitment.

What's the point of view? It's written in first-person point of view, but how did Fielding make that choice? We can't know for sure, so let's ask the question a little differently. Why does first-person point of view make sense? It's the best choice because the narrative device is Bridget's diary, and when people write in a diary, they typically write in first-person point of view for themselves. In this story, Bridget records the events of her life over the course of a year, and the narrative unfolds through the written entries. That's the form of the narrative.

What else can we say about the narrative device?

Bridget as the protagonist is a character within the story and she is the intended audience. She describes events shortly after they happen because she wants to track how well she is following her New Year's resolutions.

What else can this tell us about the narrative?

Diaries are meant to be private, and this tells us that Bridget is fairly forthcoming about what she's thinking and doing—at least to the extent that she's self-aware. We also can expect that she's objective about some things (for example, her mother's behavior) but may have less objectivity when it comes to herself.

She possesses some hindsight but not a lot. If she were writing about events in the distant past, she would write about them differently. Toward the end of the story, she has the benefit of greater perspective for events that happen earlier in the story. And this is significant because as Bridget changes, the way she sees earlier events changes too. The narrative device doesn't change, but Bridget's vantage point alters gradually. This makes sense because of the Worldview arc woven through the global Love Story. The ability to see herself clearly improves as external conflict forces her to see how her prior worldview does not serve her.

Let's get back to why Bridget is recording these events and how this purpose is tied to the controlling idea. Bridget's purpose in starting the diary is to record how successfully she sticks to her resolutions, but what she learns by the end of the year is the controlling idea of the story. *Love triumphs when we learn to respect ourselves.* So the controlling idea can be the lesson that flows from the narrator's experience of telling of the story, especially when they are the protagonist.

It's significant to note that Bridget as the protagonist-narrator didn't set out to tell a Love Story. That was Helen Fielding's goal. Because their goals are different, it's important to think about them differently, like nested dolls of narrative purpose. Of course, as the writer, you might agree with your story's controlling idea, and it might be your purpose to share this message, too. But your vantage point is different from the narrator's. You are the creator, a god of your story world, but it doesn't tell you how to build it and what to do with it. The specificity of your narrative device, when tied to your story's controlling idea, will help you make wise story choices to give you a better chance of delivering a satisfying experience.

Here's an example to help us understand how the narrative device helps us decide which details to include within the scenes of a story. Bridget's diary entries include how much alcohol she drinks each day and how many cigarettes she's smoked. These details often produce a comedic effect, but that alone is not a reason to include them. They are consistent with the narrative device, though. Bridget is tracking her New Year's resolutions, which includes limiting alcohol and cigarettes. And these details make sense in light of the controlling idea because Bridget's consumption is a barometer of her self-respect. If you tracked her resolution success on a line graph, it would probably look an awful lot like the Story Grid Infographic of Bridget's internal Worldview arc.

Can you see how this specificity makes Fielding's writing process easier? The details make sense in the story as written. But what if Fielding had chosen a slightly different narrative device? How might Bridget present this story differently if she wanted to share the message or controlling idea with her teenage daughter? Bridget (and therefore Fielding) would likely include different details to teach the lesson and demonstrate the change. So, without altering the genre, setting, protagonist-narrator, or the basic events of the story, change the audience and the details and how we present them should change too.

With her specific narrative device and the basic events of the story, Fielding can ask herself, what would Bridget write in her diary after experiencing these events? The diary as a narrative device gives Fielding a clear opening for each scene, and she can eliminate whole categories of information (for example, character actions, character dialogue, and details about the setting) because she knows who is telling the story, to whom, why, in what form, where, and when.

This is a useful example for a story told through a narrator, but what about a story that is shown?

7

BROOKLYN

Brooklyn is a global Status Story by Colm Tóibín about a young Irish woman in the early 1950s who seeks opportunity in Brooklyn, a very different world, where she has no family.

What's the point of view? Tóibín chose selective omniscience, which means the narration comes directly from within a character, in this case the protagonist, Eilis Lacey. Why might the writer have chosen this point of view?

One category of detail we need in a Status story that is particularly well-handled in this story are the things characters say and do that indicate where they are (or believe they are) in the social hierarchy relative to others. If these details were told instead, they could feel like too much exposition. Eilis's observations show us things that other characters don't realize they're exposing about themselves. And we're shown what Eilis thinks and what she does as a result. We know when she's holding back and when she fully expresses herself.

This effect of the narrative is similar to first-person point of view but without the character's self-conscious telling to achieve a certain purpose. The novel is written in past tense and the text includes references to Eilis's perspective that suggest the events she's discussing are in the recent past. But the point of view (and to be fair, Tóibín's masterful writing) creates the effect of immediacy. The narrative feels like a replay of her day.

But who is the audience and what's the purpose if the story is not curated or narrated? To answer, we need to look at clues in the text itself and use our imagination. The narrative feels like a mind engaged in understanding what circumstances mean to make a decision. And this makes sense given the global genre. Status stories are really about moments of crisis and decision. Of course, all stories include moments of crisis and decision, but that's not necessarily *what they are about*. Status stories zero in on the question, *what are we willing to sacrifice for success?*

What's the controlling idea of the story? In other words, what's the lesson the point-of-view character might learn from reviewing the events of the story? *We are successful when we honor our moral code, realizing we can never know if we've made the right decision.*

The quiet nature of a story like this and the choice of selective omniscience means we must be all the more disciplined in terms of structure and technical choices because it's easy to get off track. It's so easy to fall in love with the details. Gorgeous writing alone could cause us to completely miss what's truly driving the story. So while no one is consciously telling the story to another person, Eilis's whole being is fully engaged in the problems at hand. Understanding that purpose helps us distinguish between the kinds of details we need to support the story and the ones we don't.

8

THE IMITATION GAME

The Imitation Game is a 2014 historical drama directed by Morten Tyldum from the screenplay by Graham Moore. The film is based on the 1983 biography by Andrew Hodge, *Alan Turing: The Enigma*. Although it's a film, it's a useful example of the way point of view and controlling idea work together.

What's the global genre? This is a Performance Story involving the legendary mathematician. We observe the story of how Turing was an integral member of the team tasked with cracking the Enigma machine code to prevent German attacks on the Allied forces during World War II. We feel triumph when the team cracks the code, which in a way fortifies us for the harder truth that follows.

The Performance Story is framed by a Crime Story set in 1951 when Turing becomes the victim of a society that criminalizes same-sex relationships. Turing faces the problem of exposing society's crimes to the Manchester police detective Robert Nock. To do this, he tells the Performance Story.

The multiple story lines in this film offer the opportunity to explore an important question. How can we prevent society from suppressing the gifts of individuals, simply because they are different, when our combined gifts help us solve the near-impossible problems we face that threaten our survival?

What point of view did the writer and director choose? The police interrogation takes the form of Turing's first-person narrative. When we visit scenes from the past, through Turing's memories, we see them through selective omniscience. Framing the story this way allows us to experience events from two vantage points in time and through the lenses of two different content genres—in triumph as Turing and the team crack the code and in shame as a national hero is persecuted.

First person makes sense because Turing tells his story to Nock in the context of a police interview to answer the detective's question, "What did you really do during the war?" The interview happens in an interrogation room in 1951. The war is over, Turing is working in Manchester, but he is forbidden from speaking of his work to solve the Enigma machine problem.

On the surface, Turing explains his work to get himself released from custody. But the bigger purpose seems to address the story's controlling idea that combines both Performance and Crime stories: *Tyranny reigns when society is the perpetrator, using shame to suppress the gifts of individuals who would otherwise benefit society.*

The Performance Story shows us how vital Turing's gifts were to the war effort. It's estimated that the combined efforts shortened the war by two years and saved the lives of fourteen million people. Who knows what other problems Turing might have solved had he not been prosecuted for being different? And as a member of the audience, we can't help but ask, what do we risk *right now* because we haven't learned this lesson and society continues to suppress the gifts of those who are different?

The Performance Story alone would show us Turing's contribution but wouldn't offer the same message with the same impact as when it's delivered in the bigger context. Imagine if the Crime Story were reduced to a footnote at the end. We would feel the missed opportunity, but not in the same way. Multiple vantage points allow us to step back and see the real harm that happens when the gifts of individuals are suppressed.

So that's a single selective omniscient point of view story within a first-person point of view framing story. How do we analyze a story that mixes multiple points of view and vantage points in the narrative?

9

HARRY POTTER AND THE HALF-BLOOD PRINCE

Harry Potter and the Half-Blood Prince is book six of the seven-book series by J.K. Rowling. The titular protagonist is an adolescent wizard attending magical boarding school in a world with magical and non-magical domains. His primary external challenge is that the dark wizard Voldemort is bent on destroying society and holds a particular grudge against Harry because he is the "Boy Who Lived."

Expansive scope stories, like this one, typically include multiple settings and may span months or years. Each story in the series spans a school year. The setting is populated by a large cast of characters (many with strong internal arcs) and includes complicated forces of antagonism. Multiple subplots and several smaller story threads are woven through the scenes.

What's the point of view? The vast majority

of the narrative is written in selective omniscience (also called "close third") through Harry's mind. The narrative distance (between the narrator and character) here is quite close. No one is filtering Harry's experience—at least on the surface, though a narrator occasionally pops in to share information about the circumstances in the scene.

This point of view is an excellent choice in a story about young people trying to navigate adolescence in a complex environment where they face existential threats. They must learn to trust their intuition and take action because the adults aren't always listening. This is a great way to smuggle advice and information teens need that would probably be rejected if not included in an entertaining story.

So selective omniscience makes sense, but we also see instances of editorial omniscience, for example in the opening scene with the muggle prime minister, Fudge, and Scrimgeour (former and incoming ministers of magic). In that scene, the narrator has access to the prime minister's thoughts and memories. The narrative distance is still pretty close here, but it's filtered through a narrator. Rowling needed a way to catch up on what's happened since the end of the prior book and to set the stage for the coming conflict. This point of view fulfills this purpose.

The "Spinner's End" scene, with Professor Severus Snape, Bellatrix Lestrange, and Narcissa Malfoy, is presented through dramatic mode. We don't have access to anyone's thoughts—only actions and spoken words. The narrative distance is quite remote. Rowling uses this point of view when she wants to keep the characters' true motivations a secret from the reader. Here she wants to keep us guessing where Snape's loyalties lie.

What is the narrative device here? When it's unidentified, which is the case for the vast majority of third-person narration, we use our imagination and ask, what narrative device could account for these different vantage points?

What clues am I looking at? Harry's selective omniscient narration is different from Eilis's in *Brooklyn* because we receive the story from her vantage point throughout. The events are presented through her mind, for her purposes.

Given the expansive scope of *Harry Potter and the Half-Blood Prince*, and the different points of view and the range of narrative or psychic distance, the narration feels like a curated narrative. The narrator could be someone like Dumbledore (though not Dumbledore himself because of the way the series ends), years or decades in the future, with a Pensieve—the magic device that allows one character to experience the memories of others—and access to a vast library of memories.

The audience for a story like this would be a young person (or young people) facing life-threatening situations in addition to all the usual challenges that come with adolescence, which are quite enough without a powerful wizard destroying the world.

And the message? In the context of the entire series, we can see how this story sends the message that the only way to solve existential threats is for us to continuously upgrade our worldview. Is it any wonder these stories resonate with readers of all ages?

10

THE WRITER'S PERSPECTIVE

When Story Grid creator Shawn Coyne was asked about whether every story needed a narrative device, even those without a true narrator, without hesitation he said *yes*. How come? Because as a writer, you must have a perspective.

What does that mean? We aren't different from an omniscient narrator who needs a reason to tell their story. Knowing the point we want to make helps us decide which global genre is best for our story and what narrative device or controlling idea. A specific purpose helps us stay the course when we want to quit because it gets really hard.

So, what message are you trying to share? What are you willing to stand up for? And what do you refuse to put up with? Why write this story with this protagonist in this setting? It matters.

If we can't answer these questions, we'll have a hard time writing a coherent narrative—one that makes sense and integrates the action, motivation, and change of the story on the global level and in the individual scenes. The failure to be specific about our perspective is a major cause of meandering unfocused drafts as well as the ones that stay on the surface. An unfocused early draft may be an important stage to go through, but it's not a story that works and delivers a satisfying experience.

Even if we include the conventions and obligatory moments for the global genre along with Story Grid's Five Commandments of Storytelling, we'll find it hard to deliver the catharsis the reader is looking for if we don't choose the point of view and narrative device with intention. That intention comes from our individual perspective.

You have a dream to write. But why? Life is short. Writing a story that works takes time and energy you could spend doing something else. And if you're dreaming of all the money you'll make, there are far easier ways to earn a living. If you keep writing despite these hard truths, it must be because you have something to say about where we are, where we could be, and how we might get there. Figure that out and you'll be on the road to finding a fitting narrative device and point of view.

11

CONCLUSION

Now that we have this new perspective on point of view, what should we do next?

First, we need to read lots of different examples of different points of view. Read parts of the stories mentioned here or grab a collection like *Points of View: An Anthology of Short Stories* edited by James Moffett and Kenneth R. McElheny. Seeing different examples is the best way to understand how they work and the effect they create. Until we learn to spot narrative devices for ourselves, these concepts are just ideas. And if you're a novelist, there is no substitute for written stories. Point of view in films can be useful, but we need to observe the text on the page.

Ask these questions about the stories you read to analyze point of view and narrative device choices.

- What's the point of view?
- From whose perspective or what vantage point is the story revealed?
- Who is the audience, or who could the audience be?
- Why is the story being told or shown?
- When and where is the story being told or shown relative to the events of the story?
- In what form?

Next, run experiments. Point of view is not an easy fix if you realize you need to change mid-draft or once your draft is complete. When you have a likely option, take it for a test drive with some of your key scenes, particularly the core event. (This is also useful when you have trouble choosing among a few main options.) Seeing the choice in action with your specific story will help you avoid mistakes that lead to page-one rewrites.

Above all, keep leveling up your own perspective and persist.

Choosing Point of View

FLOWCHART

Why are you writing this story?

What is the best vantage point from which to present it?

What narrative device should you choose?

*Who tells or shows the story?
*To whom?
*Where and when is the story being told or shown relative to the story events?
*In what form is the story being told or shown?
*Why?

What is the effect of the narrative device?

Which point of view choice best creates this effect?

Point of View Options

Point of View

	Showing Mode		Telling Mode	
First Person "I"	**Second Person** "You"	**Third Person** "He, She, They"	**First Person** "I"	**Second Person** "You"
First Person Present Tense	Second Person Present Tense	Selective Omniscience	First Person Past Tense	Second Person Past Effect
The Hunger Games	*Bright Lights, Big City*	*Brooklyn*	**Protagonist** *Treasure Island*	"How to Be an Other Woman"
		Dramatic "Hills Like White Elephants"	**Peripheral Narrator** *Moby Dick*	

Third Person "He, She, They"
Editorial Omniscience
A Wizard of Earthsea

Multi-Person Narrative
The Guernsey Literary & Potato Peel Pie Society (Epistolary)
Ethan Frome (First person framing device with Selective Omniscience)
Pride & Prejudice (Editorial Omniscience with the Indirect)

ABOUT THE AUTHOR

LESLIE WATTS is a Story Grid Certified Editor, writer, and podcaster based in Austin, Texas. She's been writing for as long as she can remember—from her sixth-grade magazine about cats to writing practice while drafting opinions for an appellate court judge. Leslie has co-authored *The Tipping Point by Malcolm Gladwell: A Story Grid Masterworks Analysis Guide* and *What's the Big Idea? Nonfiction Condensed*, both with Shelley Sperry, and *Conventions and Obligatory Moments: The Must-Haves to Meet Audience Expectations* with Kimberly Kessler. As an editor, Leslie helps fiction and nonfiction clients write epic stories that matter. She believes writers become better storytellers through study and practice, and editors owe a duty of care to help writers with specific and supportive guidance. You can find her online at Writership.com.

ABOUT THE EDITOR

SHAWN COYNE created, developed, and expanded the story analysis and problem-solving methodology the Story Grid during his quarter-century-plus career in book publishing. A seasoned story editor, book publisher, and ghostwriter, Coyne has also co-authored *The Ones Who Hit the Hardest: The Steelers, the Cowboys, the '70s, and the Fight for America's Soul* with Chad Millman and *Cognitive Dominance: A Brain Surgeon's Quest to Out-Think Fear* with Mark McLaughlin, M.D. With his friend and editorial client Steven Pressfield, Coyne runs Black Irish Entertainment, LLC, publisher of the cult classic book *The War of Art.* Coyne oversees the Story Grid Universe, LLC, which includes Story Grid University and Story Grid Publishing, with his friend and editorial client Tim Grahl.

Made in the USA
Columbia, SC
03 November 2020